YOUR BODY SYSTEMS

The Respiratory System

by Rebecca Pettiford

BLASTOFF! READERS

3

BELLWETHER MEDIA · MINNEAPOLIS, MN

612.2
PET

Note to Librarians, Teachers, and Parents:

Blastoff! Readers are carefully developed by literacy experts and combine standards-based content with developmentally appropriate text.

Level 1 provides the most support through repetition of high-frequency words, light text, predictable sentence patterns, and strong visual support.

Level 2 offers early readers a bit more challenge through varied simple sentences, increased text load, and less repetition of high-frequency words.

Level 3 advances early-fluent readers toward fluency through increased text and concept load, less reliance on visuals, longer sentences, and more literary language.

Level 4 builds reading stamina by providing more text per page, increased use of punctuation, greater variation in sentence patterns, and increasingly challenging vocabulary.

Level 5 encourages children to move from "learning to read" to "reading to learn" by providing even more text, varied writing styles, and less familiar topics.

Whichever book is right for your reader, Blastoff! Readers are the perfect books to build confidence and encourage a love of reading that will last a lifetime!

This edition first published in 2020 by Bellwether Media, Inc.

No part of this publication may be reproduced in whole or in part without written permission of the publisher. For information regarding permission, write to Bellwether Media, Inc., Attention: Permissions Department, 6012 Blue Circle Drive, Minnetonka, MN 55343.

Library of Congress Cataloging-in-Publication Data

Names: Pettiford, Rebecca, author.
Title: The Respiratory System / by Rebecca Pettiford.
Description: Minneapolis, MN : Bellwether Media, Inc., 2020. | Series: Blastoff! Readers. Your Body Systems | Audience: Age 5-8. | Audience: K to grade 3. | Includes bibliographical references and index.
Identifiers: LCCN 2018056086 (print) | LCCN 2018057527 (ebook) | ISBN 9781618915634 (ebook) | ISBN 9781644870228 (hardcover : alk. paper) | ISBN 9781618917553 (pbk. : alk. paper)
Subjects: LCSH: Respiration–Juvenile literature. | Respiratory organs–Juvenile literature.
Classification: LCC QP121 (ebook) | LCC QP121 .P49 2020 (print) | DDC 612.2–dc23
LC record available at https://lccn.loc.gov/2018056086

Editor: Rebecca Sabelko   Designer: Brittany McIntosh

Printed in the United States of America, North Mankato, MN.

Table of Contents

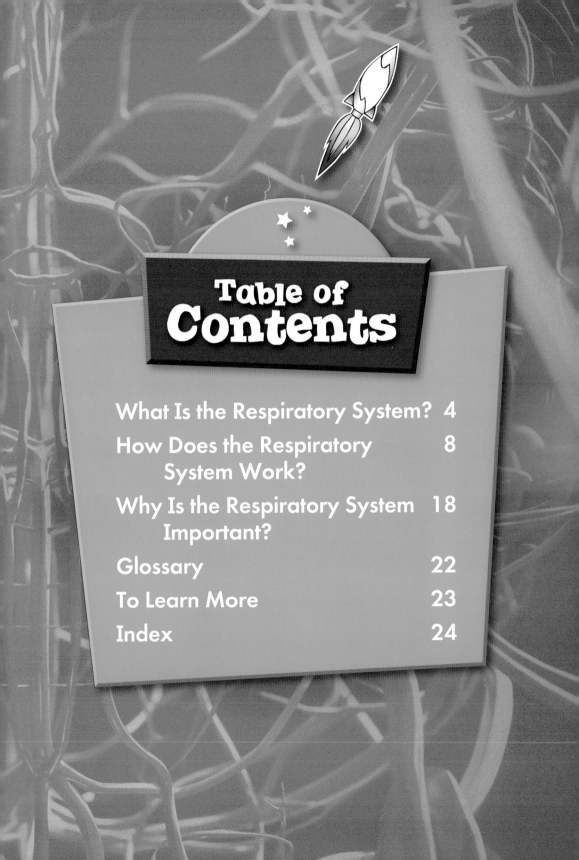

What Is the Respiratory System?

oxygen

The respiratory system brings **oxygen** into the body. It removes **carbon dioxide**.

We breathe in oxygen. The body's cells use it for **energy** and growth. Then the body makes waste. Carbon dioxide waste is breathed out.

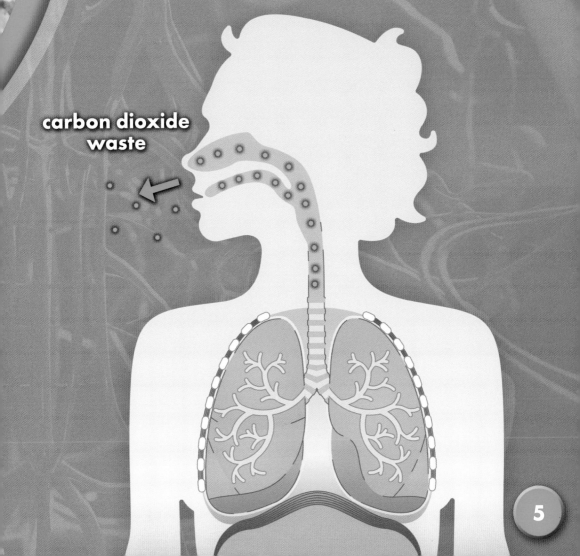

carbon dioxide waste

The respiratory system begins and ends with the airway. It includes the nose, mouth, **trachea**, and **bronchi**.

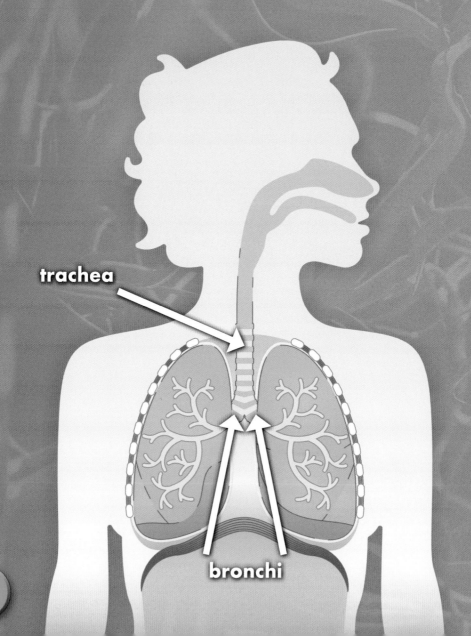

trachea

bronchi

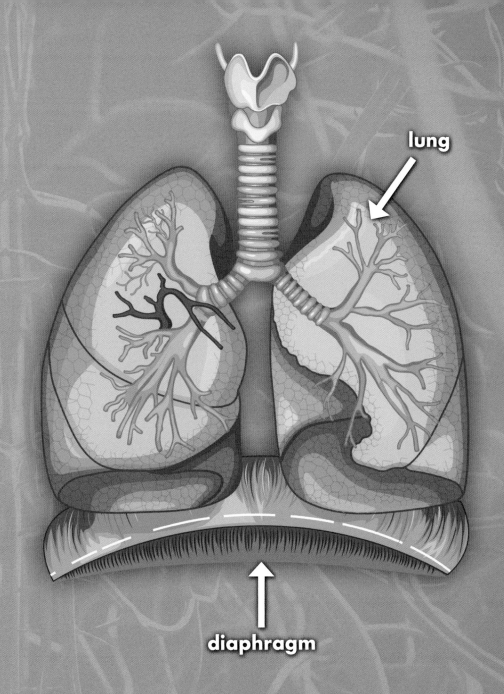

lung

diaphragm

The lungs and **diaphragm** also make up the respiratory system.

How Does the Respiratory System Work?

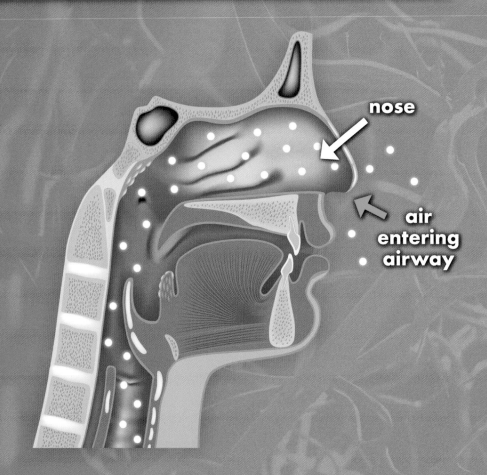

nose

air entering airway

The diaphragm **contracts** and pulls air into the nose or mouth. The air that enters the nose or mouth passes through the airway.

The air ends up in the lungs. The lungs get bigger as more air fills them.

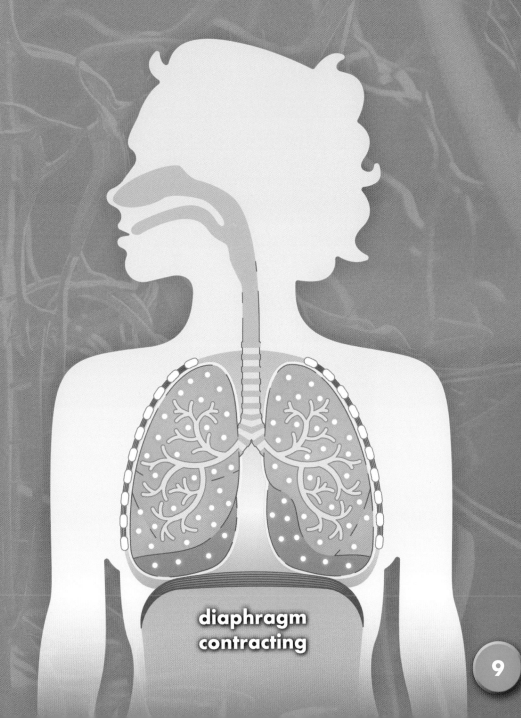

diaphragm contracting

The respiratory system is lined with a **mucous membrane**. The membrane traps things like dust and smoke. **Cilia** line the membrane. These tiny hairs move the trapped material out the nose and mouth.

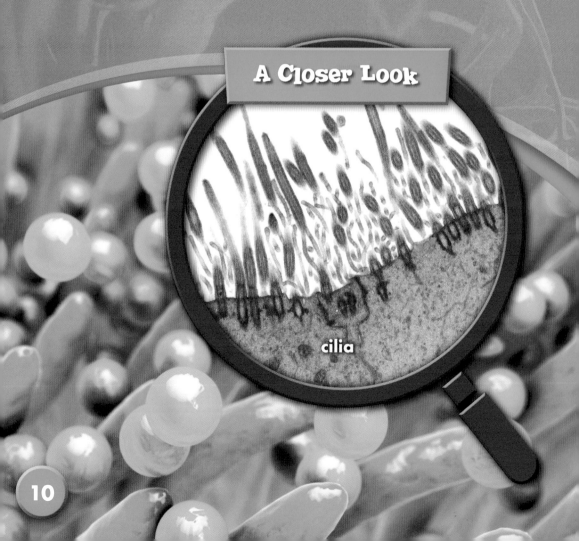

A Closer Look

cilia

dust and smoke

clean air

The clean air moves
down the trachea.

The trachea branches into two
bronchi. Air moves through these
tubes and enters the lungs.
The bronchi branch into
bronchioles. They end
with tiny air sacs.

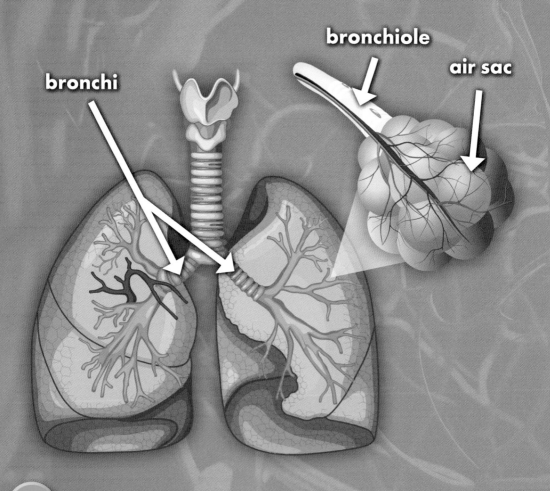

bronchiole

air sac

bronchi

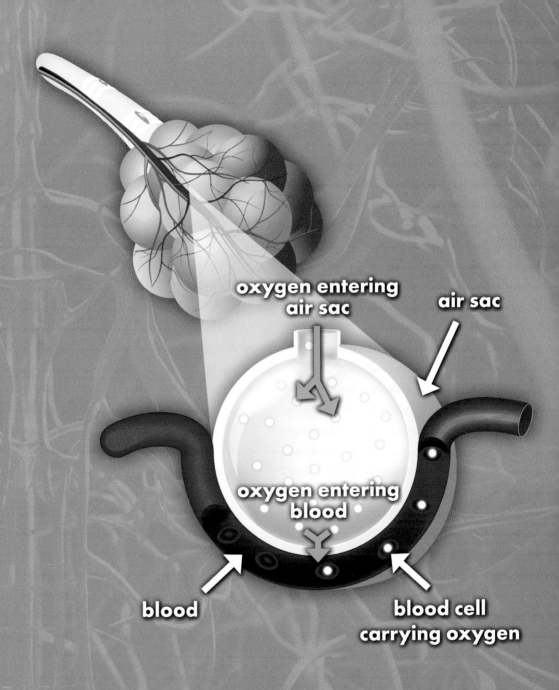

oxygen entering
air sac

air sac

oxygen entering
blood

blood

blood cell
carrying oxygen

Oxygen passes through the air sac
walls. The oxygen enters the blood.

Oxygen-rich blood leaves
the lungs. It goes to
the heart.

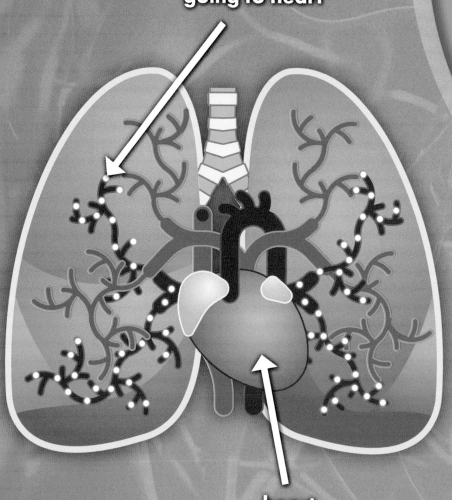

oxygen-rich blood
going to heart

heart

The heart pumps the blood through the body. The blood gives oxygen to the body's cells.

body's cells use oxygen

cells make carbon dioxide

carbon dioxide enters blood

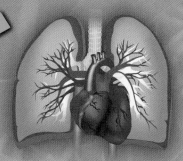

carbon dioxide enters lungs and heart

The cells use oxygen and make carbon dioxide. The blood carries carbon dioxide back to the heart and lungs.

The diaphragm pushes air out of the lungs. Carbon dioxide leaves the body.

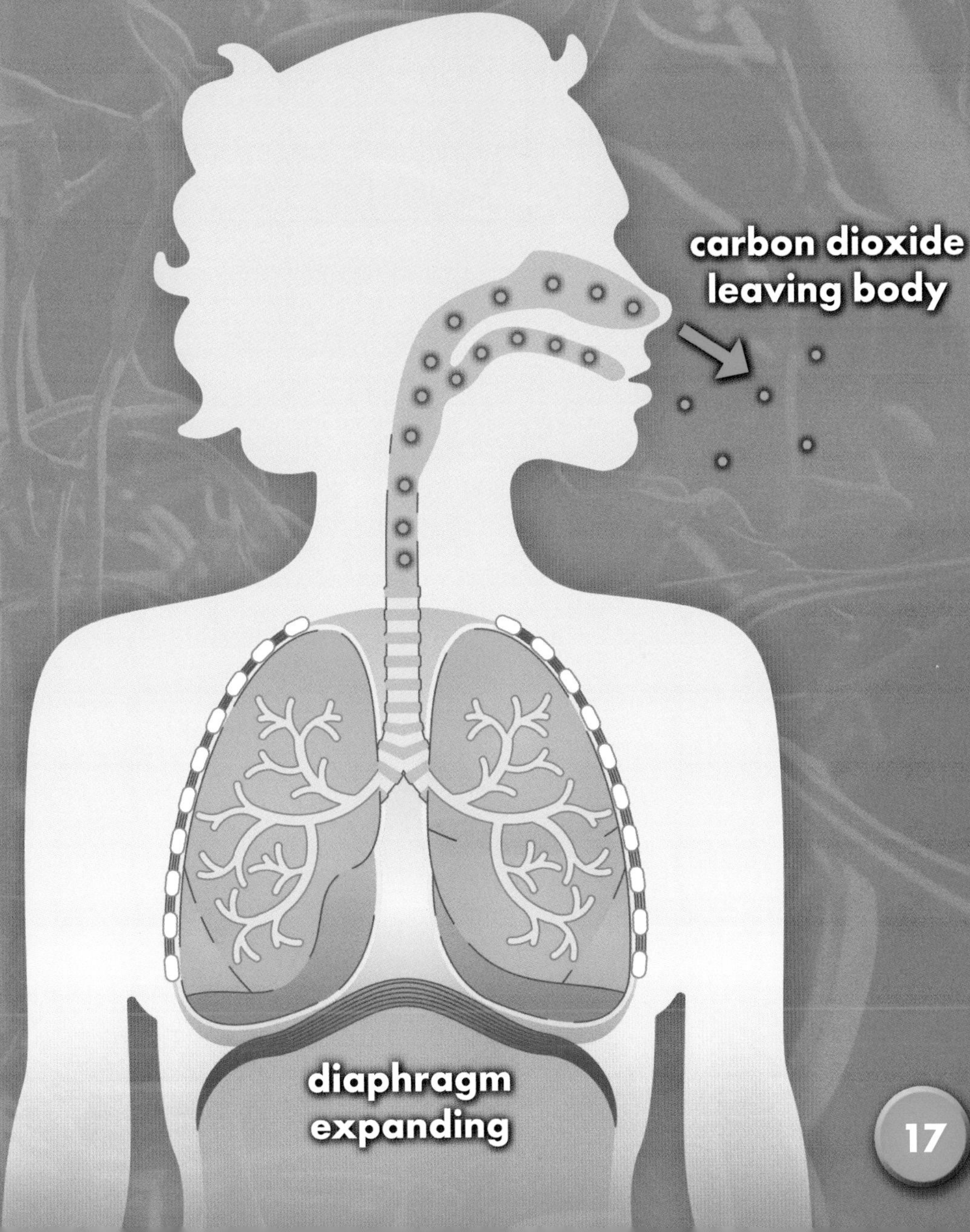

carbon dioxide leaving body

diaphragm expanding

The respiratory system also forces air between the **vocal cords**. The air makes the cords move back and forth. This makes sounds. It is why we can talk and sing!

Your Respiratory System at Work!

See how much air your lungs can hold!

You will need:
- a straw or clean plastic tubing
- a clear, 2-liter plastic bottle
- water
- a large basin

1. Fill half of the large basin with water.

2. Fill the plastic bottle to the top with water. Put the cap back on.

3. Turn the bottle upside down. Place it in the basin of water. Reach under the water to remove the bottle cap. Do not lift the bottle out of the water.

4. Push one end of the straw or tube into the open bottle.

5. Take a big breath in. Breathe out as much air as you can through the straw or tube.

The air from your lungs takes the place of the water in the bottle. The empty space in the bottle shows how much air your lungs can hold!

It is important to take care
of the lungs. Exercising
makes the lungs stronger!

Strong lungs help us breathe
every day without even thinking!

Glossary

bronchi—the two ends of the trachea that lead to the left and right lungs

bronchioles—any of the small branches from the bronchi

carbon dioxide—a gas that people breathe out; cells make carbon dioxide.

cilia—tiny hairs

contracts—shortens

diaphragm—the large, flat breathing muscle that lies under the lungs

energy—the power to move and do things

mucous membrane—a thin, wet layer of skin that is inside the airway and makes a sticky goo

oxygen—a substance in the air that is necessary for life

trachea—the main pipe air passes through

vocal cords—thin pieces of skin in the throat that help people make sound

To Learn More

AT THE LIBRARY

Kenney, Karen Latchana. *Respiratory System.*
Minneapolis, Minn.: Jump!, 2017.

Salt, Zelda. *20 Fun Facts About the Respiratory System.*
New York, N.Y.: Gareth Stevens Publishing, 2019.

Tyler, Madeline. *Why Do I Sneeze?* New York, N.Y.:
Crabtree Publishing Company, 2019.

ON THE WEB

FACTSURFER

Factsurfer.com gives you
a safe, fun way to find
more information.

1. Go to www.factsurfer.com.

2. Enter "respiratory system" into the search box
   and click 🔍.

3. Select your book cover to see a list of related
   web sites.

Index

The images in this book are reproduced through the courtesy of: mdgrphcs, front cover; Bencha Maiwat, p. 4 (left); Orange Deer studio, p. 5 (right); VectorMine, pp. 5, 6, 9, 11, 14, 17; Vecton, pp. 7, 12 (left); Alila Medical Media, p. 8; Science Photo Library/ Alamy, p. 10 (top); Kateryna Kon, p. 11 (bottom); Designua, pp. 12 (right), 13 (top, bottom); u3d, p. 15; LDarin, p. 16 (left); EgudinKa, p. 16 (top right); Studio BKK, p. 16 (bottom right); Antonio Guillem, p. 18; photka, p. 19 (left); gvictoria, p. 19 (right); Denis Kuvaev, p. 20; Adamov_d, p. 21.